COTEHELE HOUSE

Cornwall

THE NATIONAL TRUST

This is a shortened and revised version of the guidebook first published in 1991, which in turn drew on the first Cotehele guidebook written by James Lees-Milne and on subsequent editions by the late Michael Trinick. The late John Cornforth's articles on the furnishing of Cotehele in *Country Life* has also been very useful. In 2003–4 an architectural survey of the complex history of Cotehele House was undertaken by the Cornwall County Council's Historic Environment Service. The considerable cost of this was met by the National Trust's benefactors and patrons. A full copy of the report is available at the house. Tours which explain the external composition of the building can be booked in advance. The Trust also gratefully acknowledges the support of English Heritage, which has grant-aided restoration of the tapestries, of the National Art Collections Fund, and of Maureen Attrill and the staff of the City of Plymouth Museum & Art Gallery. The extract from Queen Charlotte's diary is quoted by gracious permission of Her Majesty the Queen.

© 1991 The National Trust
Registered charity no. 205847

Reprinted 1997, 2000, 2001, 2002, 2003, 2006; revised 1998, 2004, 2005, 2007, 2008
ISBN 978-1-84359-056-9

Photographs: City of Bristol Museum & Art Gallery/ Bridgeman Art Library, London p. 43; City of Plymouth Museum & Art Gallery pp. 6, 7, 37, 38, 41; City of Plymouth Museum & Art Gallery, Mount Edgcumbe House Collection pp. 1, 29, 40, 44, 46, 47, 48; Country Life Picture Library pp. 4 (left), 16, 19, 33; National Trust p. 5; NT/Robert Chapman p. 34; National Trust Photographic Library p. 39; NTPL/Andrew Besley p. 35; NTPL/Andreas von Einsiedel front cover, pp. 9, 10, 13, 15, 17, 22, 23, 24, 25, 28, back cover; NTPL/Roy Fox p. 45; NTPL/John Hammond p. 14; NTPL/Angelo Hornak pp. 11, 12, 18, 20 (left and right), 21, 26; NTPL/Stephen Robson p. 31; NTPL/Charlotte Wood p. 4 (right).

Designed by James Shurmer

Phototypeset in Monotype Bembo Series 270 by Intraspan Ltd, Smallfield, Surrey (IS291)

Printed by Hawthornes for National Trust (Enterprises) Ltd, Heelis, Kemble Drive, Swindon, Wilts SN2 2NA on stock made from 75% recycled fibre

(*Front cover*) The Hall

(*Title-page*) The coat of arms of Richard, 1st Baron Edgcumbe, who died in 1758 (City of Plymouth Museum & Art Gallery, Mount Edgcumbe House Collection)

(*Back cover*) The early eighteenth-century painted mirror in the Old Dining Room

CONTENTS

COTEHELE

This magical Tudor house, hidden away in the valley of the Tamar and even today accessible only by a network of narrow lanes, is a rare survival. Built largely between 1485 and 1560, it still preserves the great hall and solar block of the traditional medieval plan and a warren of dark and dimly lit rooms which escaped later modernisation. The house turns its back on the world, the main ranges looking inward on to three internal courtyards and only small windows piercing the exterior walls. Cornwall in the fifteenth and sixteenth centuries was lawless and unstable, with rebellions in 1497, 1548 and 1549, and great landowners still needed to build with defence in mind. Although large, Cotehele is not in any sense grand. The rough slatestone rubble and coarse granite with which it is built has an attractively rustic quality as well as a strongly regional flavour.

Cotehele's preservation is intimately connected with the fortunes and interests of the Edgcumbe family, who owned the estate for nearly 600 years from 1353 until it came to the National Trust in 1947. The present house was begun by SIR RICHARD EDGCUMBE (d.1489), who started to remodel the existing property in the last four years of his life, after being handsomely rewarded for his loyalty to Henry Tudor at the Battle of Bosworth. It was continued by his son Sir Piers (1468/9–1539), who further increased the family's wealth by marrying rich local heiresses, Joan Durnford, in 1493 and Katherine Bletsoe in 1525. In 1553 Piers's son Richard built a new house at Mount Edgcumbe overlooking Plymouth Sound some fifteen miles to the south, and this became the principal family seat. Cotehele was improved in the mid-seventeenth century, when the Royalist Col. Piers Edgcumbe moved here. However, from the end of the seventeenth century the family practically

(Far left) Sir Richard Edgcumbe (d.1489) began building Cotehele around 1485; detail from the painting of his tomb in the Chapel

(Left) George, 1st Earl of Mount Edgcumbe (1720/1–95), who helped to preserve and enhance Cotehele's ancient interiors; after Sir Joshua Reynolds

The Red Room, c.1840; one of Nicholas Condy's romantic views of Cotehele, which has changed little since

ceased to live in the house. From about this time, too, the Edgcumbes may have begun to appreciate the historic interest of Cotehele. In the late eighteenth century the preservation of Cotehele owed much to the antiquarian tastes of George, 1st Earl of Mount Edgcumbe (1720/1–95), who was a member of the Society of Antiquaries. Certainly by 1824 there were regular trips to Cotehele up the Tamar from Plymouth when parties were shown around the house. Although the east range overlooking the garden that runs down to the Tamar was remodelled in 1862 for the widow of the 3rd Earl, Caroline Augusta, this was done with a sensitivity unusual for the age. Many original features were retained, the nineteenth-century work is in complete harmony with the earlier

buildings, and the heart of the Tudor house was left undisturbed.

As a set of detailed lithographs of around 1840 after the Plymouth artist Nicholas Condy shows clearly, the house still looks very much as it was arranged at that time. Most striking is the wealth of tapestry, cut about like wallpaper to fill the spaces available, looped over doors and with little attempt to hang sets together. Yet it would be misleading to imagine that there has been continuity since the Middle Ages. Despite the strong air of antiquity, there is little of the Tudor period left in the house, and some of the seventeenth-century pieces were very probably introduced at a later date to enhance Cotehele's romantic appeal.

There is no electric light in the house, which means the rooms can be very dark on dull days. The Trust tries to be flexible in its use of sun curtains, which are essential to preserve the fragile textiles, but asks visitors to accept the home in its natural state.

TOUR OF THE HOUSE

The Exterior

THE SOUTH RANGE

The gate opens to the straight, short drive with the buttressed range of the barn built by Sir Richard Edgcumbe in 1485–9 on its right. He also built the defensive south range, with small high windows. It is shallow in plan and would have been a service range – it was only when Richard's grandson, another Richard, inserted the castellated gatehouse tower that it became the grand entrance.

THE RETAINERS' COURT

To the left of the south range lie the outbuildings of the Retainers' Court, which comprises the western part of the house. Into this court projects Sir Richard Edgcumbe's Chapel with its charming little bellcote and decorative finials, all in moulded granite. Here there is further evidence of late fifteenth-century work in the two-light, pointed windows under square dripcourses, and in the low broad west window to the Chapel. The wide pointed arch to the Hall Court, with a porter's squint beside it, was probably the original, mid-fourteenth-century entrance, approached from the north by the road from Trehill, which still exists beneath the fields around the house.

At the north end of the Retainers' Court a pointed archway leads to the Meadow, with a good

The south range, c.1840, with the Retainers' Court on the left and the barn on the right; watercolour by Nicholas Condy (City of Plymouth Museum & Art Gallery)

The Hall Court, c.1840; watercolour by Nicholas Condy (City of Plymouth Museum & Art Gallery). From left to right: the west range (leading to the Retainers' Court); the east window of the Chapel; the Great Parlour cross-wing; the Hall; and the east range

view of the north-west tower, which was added by Sir Richard Edgcumbe in the 1550s or '60s, during the same phase as the castellated gatehouse tower.

THE HALL COURT

Under the castellated gatehouse tower, a wicket door leads into the Hall Court through a narrow passage with ponderous moulded vaulting. The passageway is cobbled and just wide enough to allow a laden pack-horse to walk through it. From the court numerous archways lead to various quarters in the house, but the visitor is concerned only with the doorway immediately ahead that gives into the Hall.

A curious feature of this beautiful little court is the abrupt juxtaposition of the walls in the north-west corner. The 'squeezed in' chapel owes its appearance to the deepening and refacing of the Hall range to the south in the early 1500s, carried out by Sir Piers Edgcumbe. Below the gable are six-light windows, each in two stages, on both floors, lighting Sir Piers's Parlour (now the Old Dining Room) and the Solar (now the South and Red Rooms) above it. To the right, a similar window on the ground floor, but of four lights, marks the dais end of the Hall, which is otherwise lit by three two-light windows at a higher level under the eaves.

On the west side of the court the archway leads through to the Retainers' Court. To its left is the laundry, which was originally the porter's lodge of the old house, before Sir Richard built his new entrance tower in the south wing in the 1550s. The series of rooms above the arch was formerly a single chamber and would have been occupied by a resident chaplain.

On the opposite side of the court is the east range, the interior of which was extensively rebuilt for the 3rd Earl's widow in 1862.

The Interior

THE HALL

Unusually, the Hall is entered directly from the Hall Court rather than through a screens passage dividing it from the service rooms on the right. Although Sir Piers Edgcumbe's early sixteenth-century Hall is comparatively small, and has lost the raised dais at the western end, it is one of the most splendid interiors of the West Country and intensively evocative of the late Middle Ages, when the walls would have been hung with arms and armour ready for use in times of alarm and not merely as decoration. The floor is a rough, uneven composition of lime ash, which is soft and needs constant repair. The walls are plain and lime-washed. Over the fireplace is the seventeenth-century coat of arms of the Edgcumbe family in carved wood, which is probably funerary in origin.

ROOF

The roof is old-fashioned for the period: instead of the developed hammerbeam type, composed of massive truncated beams, it is carried on a network of smaller timbers, whose purlins are strengthened with moulded wind-braces, the total effect being light and decorative. The roof was created when Sir Piers deepened the Hall in the early 1500s. His son, Richard, dismantled the roof and re-assembled it at a higher level when he elevated the Hall range in the 1550s.

STAINED GLASS

The late fifteenth-century heraldic panes of the windows are emblazoned with the arms of the families into which the Edgcumbes married; names that evoke the past history and glories of the West Country – Holland, Tremayne, Durnford, Cotterell, Ralegh, Trevanion, Carew, St Maur, Courtenay and Fitzwalter – each contained within a diamond-shaped shield, a fleur-de-lis on the upper corner.

ARMS AND ARMOUR

It is not clear exactly when the collection was assembled here. The earliest pieces date from the late fifteenth century, but most are mid-seventeenth-century or later, and of very mixed origin. Some pieces no doubt arrived here during the Civil War, when Col. Piers Edgcumbe commanded a regiment for Charles I at Plymouth; others may have been collected by the 1st and 3rd Barons Edgcumbe in the eighteenth century. Many of the weapons seen today in the Hall can be clearly identified in J. C. Buckler's view of 1821 (on show in the Edgcumbe Room).

NORTH WALL (FACING ENTRANCE DOOR):

Above the chair, whose back folds down to form a table, is a vambrace or forearm defence, for use by a man who has lost his left hand. The fingers and thumb can be locked into place to provide a firm grip on reins or a sword. It was probably made in Germany in the seventeenth century.

There are also a pair of wheel-lock holster pistols, c.1650, a pair of eighteenth-century 'Brown Bess' flintlock muskets, English and Spanish rapiers of the seventeenth and eighteenth centuries, two crossbows, halberds and a variety of swords and firearms.

EAST (RIGHT-HAND) WALL:

The two large colours belong to the 4th (Royal South Middlesex) Militia, which was commanded by a member of the Edgcumbe family during the Napoleonic Wars. Flanking the central door are a whale's jawbones, which first appeared at Cotehele in the 1860s, and were probably put there by Caroline Augusta, the 3rd Earl's widow.

SOUTH (ENTRANCE) WALL:

The three breastplates, c.1640, are each mounted below lobster-tail helmets of the same date. The various weapons include an Elizabethan pole-arm, two tulwars (Indian sabres), a pair of Indian forearm swords, c.1800, an early pole-arm, possibly fifteenth-century, and a Zulu skin shield, with accompanying spear. To the left of these is a North African powder flask.

WEST (LEFT-HAND) WALL:

Above the early seventeenth-century oak press cupboard is a figure wearing English half-armour, c.1600. The Civil War helmets are funerary pieces, adapted to hang above tombs.

The Hall

The Old Dining Room

FURNITURE AND PEWTER

The furniture is mainly oak of the seventeenth century, with little concession to comfort, but some of it elaborately carved. The armchair with the head of a bearded man in a medallion in the back panel is a Victorian composite piece, incorporating earlier pieces. The pewter plates and mugs on the central refectory table are mainly mid-eighteenth-century, and the plates bear the coat of arms of the Edgcumbe family.

The door beyond the fireplace leads to the foot of the main staircase over a cobbled floor uncovered in 1956. Turn left into the Old Dining Room.

THE OLD DINING ROOM

The room was created by Sir Piers Edgcumbe as his principal Parlour in the early sixteenth century, where he would have dined with his family and guests; communal eating in the Hall was already in decline by this date. It seems to have assumed its current shape following the remodelling of the west range in 1650–1. The room acquired its present name after the rebuilding of the east wing in 1862. By about 1880 it had become a sort of writing-room or study, with two of the curious folding tables, thought to have been made on the estate in the seventeenth or early eighteenth centuries, brought into the centre of the room for the purpose. As antiquarian interest in the house and its contents grew in the latter half of the nineteenth century, photographs show that constant small changes were made to the arrangement and use of the showrooms. This seems peculiar as the Dowager Countess was not resident in this part of the house, dwelling instead in the east range remodelled for the convenience of daily living.

TAPESTRIES

The first of many panels of tapestry at Cotehele is encountered in this room. Here, and in subsequent rooms, they cover almost every inch of wall, and over the years have been treated more as practical wall coverings than as works of art. Hence they have been ruthlessly cut and rejoined or looped over doors and overlapped to suit the space which they had to fill. Most of the sets are no longer complete, if indeed they ever were, and many are split between several rooms. (*A comprehensive history and description of the tapestries and other textiles is also available.*)

RIGHT OF ENTRANCE DOOR:

Orpheus and Eurydice
Antwerp, *c.*1700

OVER FIREPLACE:

The Story of Circe
Antwerp, probably 1680s
The young King Picus is out hunting and is about to be transformed into a woodpecker for refusing to become Circe's lover. This tapestry has been cut down to form the equivalent of a Georgian overmantel picture or plaster relief, which suggests that this was done in the eighteenth century.

OTHER WALLS:

Pastoral scenes with Diana and Apollo
Antwerp, *c.*1675–1700

UNDER WEST WINDOW (OPPOSITE ENTRANCE DOOR):

Fragment of border
Evidently commissioned by the Edgcumbe family since it bears the family's boar's head crest.

FLOOR

The old boarded floor being rotten, it was replaced with cement after the Second World War, and the

Eurydice poisoned by a snake; Antwerp tapestry, c.1700 (Old Dining Room)

The William and Mary high-back settee in the Old Dining Room is upholstered in silk velvet with needlework panels

present elm boarding was laid in 1977. The carpet, which is not indigenous to the house, is from Donegal.

FURNITURE

The furniture is a mixture of seventeenth- and eighteenth-century pieces, and includes a rare William and Mary high-back settee upholstered in silk velvet with needlework panels. By the fireplace is a little sixteenth-century French chair of walnut, heavily carved with a scene from the story of Susannah and the Elders. The mirror painted with cavorting cherubs in a walnut frame, c.1700, on the wall opposite the fireplace is French or Italian.

CLOCK

The bracket clock is a one-handed lantern clock, dated 1668, by George Harris of Fritwell, Oxfordshire. The crude pine case is of a later date.

CERAMICS

On the central table are two rare tin-glazed earthenware dishes from the Lambeth factory painted in majolica colours and dated respectively 1670 and 1673. The blue-and-white dishes on the small tables are Delft, of the kind described by Queen Charlotte on her visit to Cotehele in 1789 (see p. 44). The soup tureen is 'Bristol Delft'.

By the large windows a door on the right leads to the Chapel.

THE CHAPEL

This was remodelled by Sir Piers in the early sixteenth century to replace one dedicated to SS Cyricus and Julitta (a common dedication in Cornwall), which had been erected by Peter Edgcumbe and licensed by the Bishop of Exeter on 12 May 1411. Piers' roof is barrel-vaulted with wooden ribs bearing decorative bosses at the intersections; including the Tudor rose, the Green Man and triple hare motif, known locally as the 'Tinner's rabbits'. A notable feature is the contemporary oak screen with carved cusped heads to the openings. The delicate tracery above the panels is thought to be mid-eighteenth-century embellishment, the cresting a Victorian addition. Many of the original chapel fittings survive, although they underwent restoration in the nineteenth century.

As well as the low broad west window for the benefit of retainers outside, there are three other views, or 'squints', into the Chapel – a narrow slit from the small room which adjoins to the south, and two from rooms on the first floor, one opening from the Solar (now called the South Room) and the other from the Priest's Room (not open to the public).

STAINED GLASS

The east window was restored in about 1880 by Fouracre & Watson of Plymouth, for little save the coat of arms and the figure of St John had escaped damage. The heraldic panels show the coats of arms of the families of Tremayne, Holland and Durnford, with whom the Edgcumbes married. In the south window the figures of St Catherine on the right and St Anne and the Virgin Mary on the left are thought to be by Anglo-Flemish glaziers working in Southwark or London, c.1520–30.

The Chapel

FLOOR

The floor retains some of its sixteenth-century tiles. The green and white glazed tiles in the chancel are early nineteenth-century, attempting to imitate the original colours of the Tudor tiles in the nave.

TEXTILES

ABOVE WEST WINDOW:

The Adoration of the Magi
Flemish, early seventeenth-century

ON SOUTH NAVE WALL BELOW WINDOW:

The early sixteenth-century altar frontal is an exceptionally fine piece of English embroidery. It bears the arms of Sir Piers Edgcumbe (1472–1539) and his wife, Joan Durnford (d.1525). The canopied figures depict Christ and the twelve Apostles, on dark crimson velvet.

FURNITURE AND FURNISHINGS

The wooden lectern is a made-up piece, probably dating from the late eighteenth century, ornamented with fragments of sixteenth- and seventeenth-century wood carvings. Some of the linenfold pew ends may have come from the Chapel in the Wood (see p. 33).

On either side of the altar stands a pair of seventeenth-century Italian walnut torchères, elaborately carved with figures of Our Lord and Saints. The silver candlesticks which stand upon them, each engraved with an image of the Archangel Raphael, are probably Flemish, *c.*1700.

MEMORIALS

Caroline Augusta, Countess of Mount Edgcumbe
(1808–81)

Lieutenant Piers Edgcumbe (1914–40)
Killed in action at Dunkirk. It originally hung in the Chapel at Mount Edgcumbe and when this was dismantled, his sister Lady Hilaria Gibbs asked that it be installed at Cotehele.

Caroline Cecilia, Countess of Mount Edgcumbe
(1839–1909)
She married the 4th Earl in the Chapel in 1906.

Kenelm, 6th Earl (1873–1965) *and his wife, Lilian*
(d.1964)
It was thanks to the 6th Earl that Cotehele came to the National Trust.

The Crucifixion; Flemish, early sixteenth-century (Chapel)

Mrs Sheila Breen
Wife of Stanley Breen of Cotehele Farm, who was organist in the Chapel. She made the replacement cover for the 'Queen Anne's tatting' chair in the Punch Room.

PICTURES

ON ALTAR:

FLEMISH, late sixteenth-century
Triptych, with the Adoration of the Magi and two donors
Panel
Dated (on the wings) 1589
The wings contain portraits of the donor and his wife, with their respective ages, 34 and 28, and what would seem to be his merchant's mark above both. The central panel, which bears the initials L.B. (possibly an attempt to pass this off as the work of

the Bruges painter-designer, Lancelot Blondeel), may not be the original, as it is painted in a quite different technique, and the three elements could have been framed together some time later to make a suitable devotional object.

SOUTH CHANCEL WALL:

FLEMISH, early sixteenth-century
The Crucifixion
Panel
Recent restoration has revealed the quality of this attractive work – especially in the landscape. It was probably painted in Antwerp, from the early sixteenth century the commercial centre, not just of the Netherlands, but of the Spanish Empire, and a magnet for most Flemish artists.

WEST NAVE WALL:

ENGLISH, eighteenth-century
The tomb of Sir Richard Edgcumbe at Morlaix
Panel
Sir Richard Edgcumbe died fighting for Anne of Brittany in 1489, and it is in Brittany that he was buried. The panel appears to have been based on the watercolour that now hangs on the main staircase. John Cornforth has suggested that the 1st Earl of Mount Edgcumbe may have had it painted for the Chapel in the Wood built by Sir Richard and restored by the 1st Earl in 1769.

CLOCK

In the south-west corner is the clock probably installed by Sir Piers in the early sixteenth century. This rare survival is the earliest domestic clock in England still unaltered and in its original position. It is a pre-pendulum clock made entirely of hand-wrought iron and mounted on a stout vertical oak support, set in a shaft built in the thickness of the wall. This shaft connects with the bellcote above, which contained two bells, one to toll for services and the other to strike the hours. The tolling bell had disappeared long since and was replaced by the National Trust with a bell from Doyden in the parish of St Minver in 1966. The striking bell is original to the house.

The clock, which has no face, is still in working order and is kept in use during the season. The machinery is controlled by a verge escapement and foliot balance (the mechanism which preceded the more accurate pendulum escapement), and was originally driven by two iron weights, each of

The Chapel clock was probably installed by Sir Piers in the early 1500s and is the earliest known example to remain in its original condition and position

about 90lb which have since been replaced. The timing can be controlled by two small moveable weights attached to the arms of the bow-shaped foliot balance which moves horizontally, as opposed to the vertical axis of the rest of the mechanism. It was overhauled in 2002 to celebrate the Queen's Golden Jubilee.

The visitor returns to the Old Dining Room where a door left of the entrance leads to the Punch Room.

THE PUNCH ROOM

The room takes its present name from the panels of tapestries depicting scenes of Bacchic revelry concerned with the making of wine. The nineteenth-century brick wine bins in a closet in the far left-hand corner also suggest that wine was drunk here. The room was known as the Little Parlour in Condy's copy of a plan dated 1731, implying that it was originally a room of some intimacy. However, it was entitled the Ante-Room in the accompanying lithograph and arranged formally with furniture against the walls. It may perhaps have acted for a

The Punch Room

period as a reception room serving the bedroom beyond, as was common practice in houses of the late seventeenth and eighteenth centuries. Like the Old Dining Room and the rooms above in the west range, it seems to have been remodelled in 1650–1. John Cornforth has suggested that the cornice and the fireplace may date from the eighteenth-century re-creation of the ancient interiors.

CARPET

This is a Persian 'Mahal' carpet, not indigenous to the house.

TAPESTRIES

The tapestries depicted by Condy are mostly from the *Liberal Arts* series now hung in different rooms, so the present panels cannot have been hung here before 1840.

The Bacchanals
English, 1670s–'80s
The Bacchanals were the infant servants of Bacchus, Roman god of wine.

OVER DOOR TO STAIRS:

A section of tapestry border, with an early Edgcumbe crest at the centre. The effect is very similar to an eighteenth-century plaster or carved wood frieze.

FURNITURE

The set of mid-eighteenth-century chairs, with their distinctive knotted wool upholstery, now comprises the principal furnishing of the room. The upholstery, which was also applied to the settee and the two pole-screens, is known locally as 'Queen Anne's tatting'.

The rest of the furniture is seventeenth-century. The two-tier oak court cupboard was made in England in the early seventeenth century and was in the Old Dining Room until at least 1840.

VESSELS

Most of the vessels and candlesticks shown in the Condy view are no longer in the house, though there are some interesting survivals including two copper ale-warmers, a lignum-vitae wassail bowl and some ornate seventeenth-century Delft vases.

The granite stairs lead to the White Room.

THE WHITE ROOM

The White Room forms the ground floor of the tower added to the house in the mid-sixteenth century and was named after the curtains and bed-hangings.

CEILING

The White Room is the only one in the house to have a decorative ceiling. It is formed of moulded wooden ribs in a geometrical pattern, pinned to the ceiling and serving no structural function. Previously considered to be seventeenth-century, the ceiling decoration may be an example of mid-eighteenth-century antiquarianism.

The White Room

A detail of the eighteenth-century crewel-work bed-hangings in the White Room

TAPESTRIES

ON RIGHT-HAND WALL:

The Bacchanals
English, 1670s–'80s
Part of the series in the Punch Room.

ON LEFT-HAND WALL:

Pygmalion
Antwerp or London, 1670s–'90s

OVER GRANITE STAIRS AND FIREPLACE:

Fragments from *Venus and Phaon*
Antwerp or London, 1670s–'90s

BESIDE FIREPLACE:

Fragment from *Liberal Arts* series
Antwerp, 1660s–'70s

BEHIND BED:

Caesar Augustus
Antwerp, 1660s–'70s

BED

The walnut bed is probably Goanese and may have been acquired through the flourishing Portuguese trade with Plymouth (Goa was a Portuguese colony until 1961). The bed-hangings, like the window curtains, are of eighteenth-century crewel-work embroidered on to a linen backing. The bedspread is of fine eighteenth-century Broderie de Marseille.

FURNITURE

The set of ebonised high-back chairs, *c.*1690, has lost the embroidered seats shown in the Condy view of the room. The beautifully figured early eighteenth-century walnut secretaire to the left of the principal window is still in the same position as it was in 1840. The mirror on the wall opposite the bed has an unusual surround of embroidered stumpwork, including a duck on a pond and a jaunty lion, and is signed and dated 'Margaret Hall 1668' on the reverse.

The door right of the fireplace leads to the Lower Landing.

THE LOWER LANDING

FURNITURE

Outside the White Room is a late sixteenth-century French oak cabinet, richly carved with architectural motifs, and biblical and mythological figures. There are also here two Welsh chairs of elaborately turned ash with triangular seats. From the late eighteenth century they were avidly collected for their curiosity value, especially by members of Horace Walpole's circle, as they were often supposed to be of monastic origin. Certainly the type existed by the mid-Tudor period, if not earlier.

The grenade-like glass bottles in a wire frame are Victorian fire extinguishers.

Turn right up the staircase; left is the Red Room.

THE RED ROOM

The Red Room together with the Upper Landing and South Rooms originally formed a single chamber, with a common roof supported by three tiers of arched braces similar to those in the Hall, but now hidden by the ceiling; it was quite common to find great chambers on the first floor open to the roof in West Country manor houses. Served by a single west-facing window, the room is naturally gloomy, but this serves only to enhance its rather

The Red Room, with the South Room beyond

mysterious atmosphere. The cracked and dirty plaster ceilings and the broad rough pine floorboards which are invariably seen in Condy's illustrations still survive in this and the adjacent room.

TAPESTRIES

LEFT OF FIREPLACE, AND FLANKING SOUTH ROOM DOOR:

Children's Games
Antwerp, 1660s – '70s

BEHIND ENTRANCE DOOR:

The Death of Remus from *Romulus and Remus* series
Brussels, 1660s

BED

The Red Room is dominated by the large bed which gives it its name. The bed curtains and valances, dating from *c.*1670, are of napped wool. The valances are decorated with intricate 'passementerie' – pieces of vellum, or parchment, and wire ornamented with silk and metal thread. The elaborate cup-shaped finials have wire branches with applied rosettes. Like many others, the arrangement and atmosphere of the room may have been a deliberate eighteenth-century creation.

FURNITURE

The furniture is the same mixture of late seventeenth- and eighteenth-century pieces, and includes an unusual travelling desk of Spanish origin dating from *c.*1660. The inlaid flowers are later

The mid-eighteenth-century crewel-work bedspread in the South Room

The South Room linen bed-hangings are embroidered in wool

embellishments. It is mounted on a plain gate-leg stand. The tall black-painted chairs on scrolled legs are of about 1680, one type with carved back-splats and the other with an upholstered back. The chair covers are watered worsted wool cloth. They can be seen in Condy's view of the room (p. 5), together with the sofa of about 1720. The Red Room is much as Condy showed it about 150 years ago.

Beyond the Red Room is the South Room.

THE SOUTH ROOM

The principal private room or 'Solar' of Sir Piers Edgcumbe's house, it was known as the Best Bed-room to Condy. With its large multi-paned south-facing window it makes a surprising contrast to the gloominess of the preceding room. The squint allowing the lord to view into the hall was a feature of many medieval and Tudor houses. However, Cotehele's may not be original – it could have been added in the eighteenth century to enhance the house's romantic appeal. The small chamber with a window into the chapel was possibly a latrine serv-ing the former Great Chamber.

TAPESTRIES

FROM LEFT TO ENTRANCE DOOR:

The Rape of the Sabines, Romulus and Remus dividing the Robbers' Spoils and *The Building of Rome* from the *Romulus and Remus* series
Brussels, 1660s

OVER FIREPLACE:

Augustus sacrifices to the 'Unknown God' from *Caesar Augustus* series
Antwerp, 1660s–'70s

BETWEEN BED AND ENTRANCE DOOR:

Numa Pompilius
Antwerp, 1660s–'70s

BED

The plain bedstead with front posts of sycamore wood is hung with a beautiful cloth of white linen embroidered in red wool in a delicate flowing design, dating from the second half of the seven-teenth century. The original ground fabric has mostly worn away and the design has been skilfully attached to the lining with a fine running stitch. The mid-eighteenth-century bedspread is of light crewel-work on a twill backing.

'Geometry' tapestry; Antwerp, 1660–'70s (Upper Landing)

TEXTILES

The Condy view of the room shows a set of matching covers for chairs and stools of different dates. These can probably be identified with the Genoese cut velvet which survives on a set of six mid-seventeenth-century chairs in the room today.

Return through the Red Room to the Upper Landing.

THE UPPER LANDING

FURNITURE

The oak cupboard front, previously believed to be a tester or ceiling board for a four poster bed, is inscribed in Welsh, which translates as: 'The expert who made it(:) Harry ap Griffith'. The board is interesting, both for its heraldic content and its biblical symbolism. The two wide and short panels in the centre replaced what would have been the drawer fronts. Two of the eight panels into which it is divided formed the doors of the cupboard: firstly, the central top panel representing the Tudor Royal Arms with the French fleur-de-lis in the second and fourth quarters, which were not formalised until 1707; secondly, the central bottom panel, which represents *The Expulsion of Adam and Eve from the Garden of Eden*. The corner panels depict, at top left, *The Instruments of the Passion*; at top right, *Musicians playing Welsh Instruments* (representing Harmony); at bottom left, *St George and the Dragon*; at bottom right, *A Woman, a Lamb, and a Dragon standing before a Fortress with a Group of Kings and Courtiers*. The frame of the cupboard front, carved in shallower relief, depicts scenes of hawking and hunting.

TAPESTRY

Geometry from the *Liberal Arts* series
Antwerp, 1660s–'70s

The Old Drawing Room

CERAMICS

The blue-and-white Chinese porcelain tray painted with a group of Roman deities is copied from a celebrated silver bas-relief known as the Corbridge Lanx, which was discovered in 1735 in the River Tyne, near Newcastle, on land belonging to the Duke of Somerset, whose arms consequently appear on the rim of the tray.

At the end of the Upper Landing on the right, a massive granite arch leads on to the Tower Stairs, and the mid-sixteenth-century tower added by Sir Richard Edgcumbe (c.1499–1562).

THE OLD DRAWING ROOM

The stout oak door, which leads into the entrance lobby of the room, features marigolds set in diamond-shaped panels. The inner porch of linen-fold carving is original to the building of the tower in the mid-sixteenth century.

The Drawing Room retained its name after the old Victorian replanning, but it was designated 'Old' to distinguish it from the New Drawing Room in the remodelled east range, and its function seems to have shrunk to that of a private bed/sitting-room, and the concession to Victorian taste is seen in its looser arrangement rather than in the introduction of new pieces.

TAPESTRIES

OVER FIREPLACE:

Romulus and Remus before Numitor from *Romulus and Remus* series
Brussels, 1660s

From *The Story of Mankind* series
Brussels, 1630s

LEFT OF INNER LOBBY, BEHIND PORCH:
Triumph of Virtue

ON OPPOSITE WALL, IN LEFT-HAND CORNER:
Temperance and the Gods

ON SAME WALL, IN RIGHT-HAND CORNER:
Time driving away the Pleasures from Age

RIGHT OF FIREPLACE:
Ceres, Bacchus and Venus

FURNITURE

George III and Queen Charlotte were entertained to breakfast at Cotehele during a visit in August 1789, and two cushions of maroon velvet were inscribed, unusually in ink, to commemorate the event. The ebony settee on which it is believed the Royal couple sat is part of a large set of furniture in this room whose mysterious origin and exotic appearance excited antiquarian interest from the eighteenth century when Horace Walpole acquired a set for Strawberry Hill. Even into this century such furniture was thought to be of Tudor origin, although the earliest examples are now considered to date from the first quarter of the seventeenth century, possibly made in Ceylon or Batavia (now Djakarta) in Indonesia, following Dutch or Portuguese prototypes.

Other furniture includes, against the long wall, a Dutch wall cabinet made about 1710. Inlaid with ebony and ivory stringing and fitted with an architectural interior recess on a later English stand, it is the most elaborate of the several cabinets and writing-desks of this period in the house. An Italian cabinet with an architectural interior, but of altogether different style and date, is in the corner of the opposite wall. Dating to about 1600, it is carved in very high relief with human figures at the angles and bearded masks at the feet, and was later ebonised to give it a particularly rich appearance. The piece figures prominently in Condy's view of the room, as does the set of ebony seat furniture. The room also contains a cedar wood chest and a Burgomaster chair.

Continue up the staircase to Queen Anne's Room.

QUEEN ANNE'S ROOM

BED

Decorated with early Tudor carved, gilt and painted posts, but with seventeenth-century finials and headboard, it is now only partially hung, the curtain material being an early eighteenth-century woollen damask, and the much damaged valances of late seventeenth-century yellow silk. The figurine surmounting the headboard is an early eighteenth-century doll. The silk patchwork quilt is Victorian.

TAPESTRIES

RIGHT OF BED:
Sacrifice of Iphigenia
Dutch, c.1650

LEFT OF BED:
Hunting Scene
Flemish, late sixteenth–early seventeenth-century

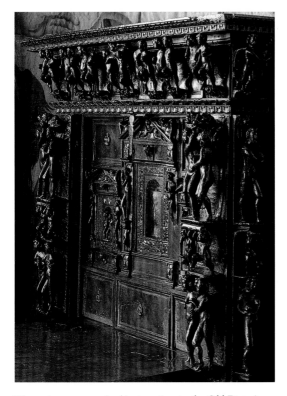

The walnut-veneered cabinet, c.1600, in the Old Drawing Room is richly carved with Adam and Eve and other figures

Queen Anne's Room

King Charles's Room

KING CHARLES'S ROOM

The room takes its name from the belief that Charles I slept here in September 1644 on his march from Liskeard to Exeter though some antiquaries believed the name referred to Charles II. Reverend Malan wrote in 1894, 'Strangers are shewn into a room, in which, that disgrace to Royalty, Charles the II passed some nights'. It is perhaps the room in the house most evocative of genuine antiquity, and there is little reason to suppose that its essential furnishing has altered since its creation in the early seventeenth century, although the bed has changed position several times.

TAPESTRIES

From *Hero and Leander* series
Mortlake, 1670s–'80s

BEHIND BED HEAD:
Leander taking leave of his Parents

BETWEEN WINDOWS:
Leander swimming the Hellespont

LEFT OF BED:
Hero mourning Leander's Death

OVER FIREPLACE AND AROUND DOORS:
Grammar and Arithmetic from *Liberal Arts* series
Antwerp, 1660s–'70s

Leander swimming the Hellespont; from the Mortlake tapestry, 1670s–'80s, in King Charles's Room

BED

It is a complicated construction, made up apparently of bulbous Elizabethan posts from a table and a seventeenth-century headboard. The late seventeenth- or early eighteenth-century hangings are of crewel-work with some silk in cross-stitch and *petit point*. The woollen backing is twentieth century.

MIRROR

The mirror on the chest by the far window, dating from about 1625, has a polished metal plate, since looking glass was extremely rare before the mid-seventeenth century.

Descend the staircase to the Lower Landing.

THE MAIN STAIRCASE

The stairs are lit by three windows overlooking the Kitchen Court in the centre of the house.

PICTURES

TO LEFT OF RED ROOM DOOR:

FRISIAN, *c.*1590
Sir Thomas Coteel
Panel
The sitter, who is identified both in the *cartellino* (painted scroll) and on a letter on the table addressed to him in London, was the father of Mary, the second wife of Sir Richard Edgcumbe (*c.*1570–1638). He was a merchant from Brabant who fled from the Spanish Inquisition towards the end of the sixteenth century – presumably shortly after this portrait was painted. The similarity of his surname and the name of the house is coincidental.

ON STAIRS, LEFT-HAND SIDE:

The tomb of Sir Richard Edgcumbe at Morlaix
Watercolour on vellum
Sir Richard Edgcumbe died fighting for Anne of Brittany in 1489 and was buried at Morlaix. His tomb was destroyed in the French Revolution, but had previously been copied in this watercolour, which seems to have provided the source for the panel painting in the Chapel.

ENGLISH, *c.*1670
Mary Glanville, Mrs Piers Edgcumbe
Oval
Daughter of Sir John Glanville (1586–1661) of Tavistock, King's Sergeant and Speaker of the Short Parliament. She was married to Col. Piers Edgcumbe, MP, but widowed in 1667. Their son, Sir Richard Edgcumbe, was the father of the 1st Baron.

ON STAIRS, RIGHT-HAND SIDE:

ENGLISH, ?eighteenth-century
Reputed portrait of Margaret Edgcumbe, Lady Denny (1560–1648)
Panel
The daughter of Sir Piers, or Peter, Edgcumbe, MP (by 1536–1607/8) and Margaret Luttrell of Dunster, and married to Sir Edward Denny (d.1599), younger son of Henry VIII's favourite, Sir Anthony Denny. She was Maid of Honour to Queen Elizabeth I, to whom her husband was Gentleman of the Bedchamber. This portrait appears to be a later pastiche.

ENGLISH, 1608
Portrait of an Unknown Man (? Sir Richard Edgcumbe)
Panel
Inscribed: *Aet suae 33 An Dieu 1606*, and with four lines of French verse
Perhaps Sir Richard Edgcumbe (1563–1638), the brother of Margaret, Lady Denny. His first wife was Anne Carey of Cockington, and his second Mary, daughter of the shadowy Flemish merchant in London, Sir Thomas Coteel.

OVER OLD DINING ROOM DOOR:

After Sir PETER LELY (1618–80)
Sir Richard Edgcumbe, KB (1640–88)
Oval
Dubbed a Knight of the Bath (whose sash he wears) before the coronation of Charles II, no doubt in recognition that his father, Col. Piers Edgcumbe, MP, had been 'a lover of the King and Church,

which he endeavoured to support, in the time of the Civil Wars, to the utmost of his power and fortune' (in the words of his monument). He was married to Lady Anne Montagu, second surviving daughter of the 1st Earl of Sandwich; their only surviving son became the 1st Baron Edgcumbe. Lely's original is at Mount Edgcumbe.

At the foot of the Main Staircase, in the cobbled Lobby, turn left into the Kitchen Court.

THE KITCHEN COURT

Leading off the foot of the stairs, this is the smallest of Cotehele's three courts and lies in the centre of the house. To the east and south are the Kitchen and Hall chimneys; to the north-west the top of the tower rises above the roofs.

The fine lead tank, bearing the initials 'TC' and the date 1639, may be connected with Sir Thomas Coteel, whose will is dated 19 June 1639.

The tapered hexagonal stones, with hollowed-out interiors, are possibly rare local types of cressets, early medieval lamps formed by a lighted wick floating in a pool of oil within the bowl. Whatever their function, one of these stones has a clear connection with Cotehele. Around its 'waist' there is inscribed ALEXANDER CHAMPNON ME FIER[I] FECIT ('Alexander Champernon made me'). Alexander Champernowne (1382–1441) owned the manor of Bere Ferrers, on the Devon side of the Tamar to the south of Cotehele. His daughter and heiress married Richard Willoughby, later Lord Willoughby de Broke, who attacked Sir Richard Edgcumbe, but later became his ally.

The large granite object, with a circular bowl cut into a rough cube, and 'lugs' projecting from its sides, apparently to enable it to be lifted, or possibly poured, is a puzzle. It is traditionally thought to be the ancient font of the house, but it is not that shown in Condy's drawing of the Chapel, lying against the foot of the lectern. Possibly the lugs were intended to be carved and the whole set upon a base. It seems more likely that it had some secular purpose.

Crossing the Kitchen Court, re-enter the house through a scullery with Victorian fittings, to reach the Kitchen.

The Kitchen

THE KITCHEN

Well placed for the Hall, the Kitchen was less well sited for the Old Dining Room, when the family ate there. The reconstruction of the east range in 1862 brought the new dining-room adjacent to the Kitchen, which continued to be used until the 6th Earl moved into the Stable House at Mount Edgcumbe in 1946. The nineteenth-century ranges, inserted in the Tudor hearth, were much broken, and in 1970 these were removed, the door from the lobby reopened and the room rearranged to accord with its appearance in the middle of the last century, as recorded by Nicholas Condy.

The principal features of the room are its great height (to allow smoke and smells to dissipate through louvred vents – now vanished), the cavernous hearth, 10 feet wide, and the immense oven in the north wall. The Kitchen was used only for cooking and baking. The storage of food, its preparation for the cook and the scouring of pots and pans were carried out in the maze of larders, sculleries and still-rooms which lead off the Kitchen Court.

The hearth is furnished with pot hooks for hanging cooking vessels over the fire, with brandises (the West Country name for a trivet) for standing pots over the embers, and with stout iron dogs slanted against the back wall, into which spits for roasting could be fitted. Above the hearth a primitive rack (the same as in Condy's drawing) holds sides of meat and bacon, salted down in the autumn for winter use.

Workers on the Edgcumbe estate taking lunch; by Nicholas Condy, c.1840 (City of Plymouth Museum & Art Gallery, Mount Edgcumbe House Collection)

The mysterious square hole in the wall to the left of the hearth may have been a putlog hole originating from the building of the medieval hall and revealed during a later building phase.

The oven, over 7 feet across and 3 feet high, and a rough oval shape, has a smaller oven beside it. It was heated by lighting a fire of dry sticks, or in poorer households of furze, which flared up quickly, giving intense heat which the walls of the oven absorbed. The ashes were raked out as the fire subsided, the food to be baked inserted and the door closed and sealed with clay. An oven of this size was essential for the large household of a Tudor squire and his retainers.

There is a formidable board of 'Rules to be Strictly Observed', including, 'That the Men at breakfast be allowed one pint of Beer or Cyder each, at Dinner and Supper Men and Maids a pint each and Strangers a quart, no other drinking whatever in the Hall or any other part of the House or out Houses under one Shilling forfeit to each offenders.' The board came to Cotehele from Honicombe, the home of the 3rd Earl's daughter, Lady Ernestine Edgcumbe, from 1905 until her death in 1925; its earlier history is unknown.

The door to the left of the hearth leads into the Lobby.

THE LOBBY

An early photograph shows that this was once an open passageway from the terrace into the house. The window and wall were added, when this entry was closed up. The curving stair to the right of the window, now blocked off, led to rooms on the upper floors used by the servants.

FURNITURE

English dial clock, made by Thos. Hill, London, c.1775.

Travelling chest, oak, with domed top, bound with patterned wrought iron, late seventeenth-century.

From the Lobby return to the Hall and leave by the main door.

THE GARDEN

HISTORY

In the late eighteenth century the 1st Earl of Mount Edgcumbe laid out an important park and garden in the Picturesque manner at Mount Edgcumbe, which were much admired by David Garrick among others. The garden at Cotehele seems always to have been more modest. In its present form it dates from around 1862, when the formal terraces on the east front of the house were laid out. The tithe maps of 1839 show that the Upper Garden and Nellson's Piece were in use as orchards, and the present Valley Garden was still wooded. In 1820 Gilbert reported that 'the wooded grounds which surround the house are of the grandest description, particularly at that part which is situated between the mansion and the river'. One of the trees was a three-trunked Spanish Chestnut (*Castanea sativa*), which had a diameter of 11 feet 5 inches before it fell in 1875, and must have been one of the biggest ever to grow in Britain. The gales of 1891, however, so badly damaged the woodlands that the house could be seen from Calstock for the first time in living memory, and it was estimated that 100,000 cubic feet of timber had fallen.

TOUR OF THE GARDEN

The garden is on many different levels. On the old grey house and the surrounding walls grow some unusual shrubs and climbers, but much of the planting is late Victorian. The Bowling Green lies above the drive which now approaches the house.

To the left the cobbled way leads through the Retainers' Court, the original entrance, with camellias on its walls. On the west wall of the Chapel is a Bushy Myrtle (*Myrtus communis*). The archway leads to the meadow at the north-west corner of the house. Nineteenth-century engravings show cows being milked here. In spring the grass is a mass of daffodils.

The doorway in the wall to the left leads to the Upper Garden with a square pond fed from a spring by a rill and planted with water lilies. On the lawn below the pond is a Golden Ash (*Fraxinus excelsior* 'Aurea' syn. 'Jaspidea') and nearby a Tulip Tree (*Liriodendron tulipiferum*). Within the yew hedges is a cutting garden to provide flowers and foliage traditionally grown in the Tamar Valley and now used in the house.

On the lawn above the pond are two young specimens of the Tree of Heaven (*Ailanthus altissima*), planted to replace a casualty of a gale in 1958. The top path runs beside a herbaceous border against a medieval wall which continues around the garden and the orchard to the south.

Another doorway, closed by a pierced fretwork door to allow a peep through, leads back into the meadow. To the right is a young Cork Oak (*Quercus suber*), planted in 1955 to replace an aged specimen on the other side of the wall, which had collapsed and later had to be removed. To the left is a doorway which leads, via a gate, into Lower Level, at the top of which is the Prospect Tower (see below). The old Judas Tree (*Cercis siliquastrum*), once below the oak, fell in the gales of January 1990; its replacement stands beyond it.

The path leads past a row of double-flowered White Thorn trees (*Crataegus oxyacantha*) and a Copper Beech (*Fagus sylvatica* 'Purpurea'). To the left of the N.W. Tower stands a group of White-beams (*Sorbus aria* 'Lutescens'). On the other side is an area now planted with Japanese maples.

Through the white gate on the left and across the lane is Nellson's Piece, until recently a market garden, but now grassed over and planted with trees and daffodils to make a place in which to sit or to picnic. A few yards up the lane a field gate leads into an enclosure where, dug into the bank, is the Ice House, in which ice from several ponds was stored for use in the summer.

The garden route, however, continues on the other side of the back drive past a Silver Weeping Lime (*Tilia paucicostata* 'Petiolaris') to the pointed arch in the north wall of the Terrace Garden. On this wall is a beautiful white wisteria (*Wisteria sinensis* 'Alba').

The three terraces were altered in 1862, when the east range of the house was remodelled. They are now planted with roses and herbaceous plants. To the left, steps lead to a tunnel under the lane which emerges at the head of the Valley Garden. The path curves down to a thatched Victorian summer-house overlooking the former medieval stewpond, where fish were kept and fed until needed. It is filled by a spring led into the 'well' below the summer-house.

Beyond the pond the path leads down the right-hand side of the valley, beside the medieval dovecote and through clumps of *Gunnera manicata*, with immense spiky flower heads in late summer.

The bottom of the valley was planted with spruces, larches and hemlocks as a barrier to shelter the garden from the cold east winds in the spring.

The shelter belt was largely destroyed by the 1990 gales and has been replanted. A gate at the foot of the path on the far (south) side leads to the small Chapel in the Wood built by Sir Richard Edgcumbe at the end of his life to mark the spot where he hid from Sir Henry Trenowth (see p. 33). The Chapel is on the riverside walk from Calstock, a mile and a half upstream, to Cotehele Quay, half a mile downstream. If the latter route is chosen, there is a steep drive from the quay which returns to the house.

The alternative is to return up through the Valley Garden, with views across the tops of the shrubs beside the stream and past the dovecote.

THE DOVECOTE

The dovecote is probably fifteenth-century, made of slatestone rubble with a corbelled roof. Inside is a 'potence' or revolving ladder, for easier access to the higher pigeon holes. Its dome-shaped roof collapsed in about 1860 and was restored by the National Trust a century later. A small family of white doves now inhabits it. The path above the dovecote turns left and emerges through a wicket gate to return to the car-park and the Barn, now the Trust's reception area, restaurant and shop.

The dovecote and Valley Garden in spring

COTEHELE AND THE EDGCUMBES

THE FIRST EDGCUMBES AT COTEHELE

Cotehele gave its name to the family who owned the estate from the latter part of the thirteenth century, and parts of the house built by the de Coteheles probably survive under later remodelling. On the death of William de Cotehele, before 1336, his two children, Ralph and Hilaria, were made wards of the lord of the manor of Calstock, John, Earl of Cornwall, brother to King Edward III. Ralph died a minor and Hilaria thus became the owner of Cotehele. In 1353 she married William Edgcumbe, declaring by petition that she would have none other. Thus Cotehele passed into the hands of the Edgcumbe family, who were to remain its owners for the next six centuries.

The Edgcumbes were of ancient Devon origin, their name deriving from Eggescombe or Edgecombe (now called Nether Edgcumbe) in the parish of Milton Abbot to the north of Tavistock. An ancient manor house still stands there, with a stone over the gateway engraved with the arms of the family, the date 1292 and the initials 'RE' for Richard Edgcumbe. Within a year of the death of William Edgcumbe in 1379/80, Hilaria married William Fleete of Sutton. They lived at Cotehele for the rest of their lives, after which it reverted to her son by her first marriage, Peter Edgcumbe.

Peter Edgcumbe seems to have died without issue, for he was succeeded by a William Edgcumbe, who appears to have been his younger brother. William represented Plymouth in the Parliament of 1446–7. For the next four centuries an Edgcumbe held a West Country seat in almost every parliament for which records survive, and the family played a central role in the politics of the region. William, in his turn, was succeeded by another Peter Edgcumbe, who married Elizabeth, daughter and heiress of Richard Holland. It was their eldest son, Richard, who was the first member of the family to achieve more than local renown.

In Cornish history Richard Edgcumbe (d.1489) has become a heroic and almost legendary figure. We first hear of him involved in a bitter feud with a neighbour, Richard Willoughby of Bere Ferrers, whose estates across the River Tamar were, oddly enough, to pass to the Edgcumbes in the late eighteenth century. As Edgcumbe was quietly riding home from a friend's house to Cotehele, Willoughby, with 34 armed men, lay in ambush to murder him, but without success. On another occasion Willoughby's armed ruffians assaulted Cotehele House, which they tried to burn, and beat one of Edgcumbe's servants 'to the hurt and damage of . . . twenty pounds and more'. In spite of these unpromising beginnings, the two men subsequently became the best of friends.

In 1483 Richard Edgcumbe, perhaps prompted by rumours that Richard III had murdered the two sons of Edward IV in the Tower of London, took the boldest step of his life by declaring himself in league against the Crown. Exeter was the rallying point for the disaffected forces under Henry Stafford, Duke of Buckingham, who was at once defeated and executed without trial. Edgcumbe, who had by then sufficiently compromised himself, was outlawed but lay in hiding at Cotehele. Here he was pursued by the King's local agent, Sir Henry Trenowth of Bodrugan, who for years past had been the terror of these parts of Cornwall. So feared and hated was he that a number of the Cornish gentry had already petitioned the King to relieve the neighbourhood of his cruelty and depredations. Trenowth soon tracked Edgcumbe to his retreat, and while he drew a cordon around the house, posted a watch at the gatehouse. Edgcumbe managed to slip through the net cast for him, and having cut the throat of a luckless sentry, fled down what is now the garden towards the river's edge, hotly pursued by Trenowth. But Edgcumbe was as

Painting in the Chapel of the tomb of Sir Richard Edgcumbe at Morlaix (d.1489), who began the re-building of Cotehele; the tomb itself was destroyed in the French Revolution

wily as he was active. With his pursuers almost upon him, he tore off his cap, put a stone into it and dropped it into the water. And so, in the words of the early seventeenth-century historian of Cornwall, Richard Carew, the pursuers, 'looking down after the noise, and seeing his cap swimming thereon, supposed that he had desperately drowned himself, and gave over their further hunting'. Meanwhile the fugitive remained hidden in the undergrowth and eventually slipped away by sea to Brittany. A few years later Edgcumbe returned and in grateful memory of this incident built upon the spot a chapel in honour of SS George and Thomas à Becket,

which still stands. It was restored in 1620 and again in 1769. It preserves a fine original doorway, resembling those which Edgcumbe built at the house, and a number of late Gothic pew ends.

In Brittany, Richard Edgcumbe joined forces with Henry Tudor and became one of his closest supporters and friends. He fought for him at the Battle of Bosworth in 1485, and, as a reward for his loyalty, was knighted and made Controller of the Royal Household when Henry became king. Nemesis finally overcame Trenowth. His estates were confiscated and given by Henry VII to Edgcumbe, who had the added satisfaction of turning the tables on his old enemy, by chasing him into the sea. The beautiful headland between Mevagissey and the Dodman, now known as Bodrugan's Leap (and also owned by the National

St Simon from the early sixteenth-century English embroidered altar frontal in the Chapel (before restoration). It bears the arms of Sir Piers Edgcumbe (d.1539) and his wife, Joan Durnford (d.1525)

Trust), commemorates the spot where Bodrugan met his death.

For the remaining four years of his life, Edgcumbe lived in great prosperity. His continued services under the Crown included an embassy in Calais to accept the allegiance of its burghers and the generalship of the royalist troops in the Battle of Stoke in 1487. In 1488 he was made Ambassador to Scotland and soon afterwards he was sent to Ireland to accept the allegiance of the local chieftains.

During the brief intervals he spent at Cotehele, Edgcumbe extended the medieval house his family had inherited from the de Coteheles (see p. 36). In 1489 he set out upon his last journey, having made his will and consigned his soul to St Thomas à Becket. He died that year at Morlaix, in Brittany, where he had gone to fight for Anne of Brittany in the company of his old neighbour from Bere Ferrers, lately created Lord Willoughby de Broke. Edgcumbe was buried at Morlaix but all trace of his tomb has vanished.

Sir Richard Edgcumbe was succeeded in his estates by his son, Piers (1468/9–1539), who was awarded the Order of the Bath at the marriage of Henry VII's elder son, Prince Arthur, to Catherine of Aragon in 1489 and was later present at the victories of Tournay, Terouanne and the Battle of Spurs. For his bravery in battle he was created knight-banneret by Henry VIII in 1513. Sir Piers was one of the leading landowners in the South West, and his first marriage, in 1493, to Joan Durnford, heiress to lands on both sides of the Tamar near Plymouth, increased his influence in the area. He tried to expand his estate still further at the Dissolution of the Monasteries in the 1530s by laying claim to Totnes Priory and Cornworthy Nunnery, which had been founded by his ancestors, but without success. The combined wealth of Sir Piers and his wife enabled him to complete his father's building operations, which lasted until his own death in 1539. His finest achievement at Cotehele is the Great Hall, in one of the windows of which appear the Edgcumbe arms impaling those of Durnford, thus suggesting that the room was finished before her death in 1525.

Among the properties which Joan Durnford brought to the Edgcumbe family was land at West

Stonehouse at the mouth of the Tamar. This later became Mount Edgcumbe, where Sir Piers enclosed the park, and in 1553 his son Richard built a new house on the estate, which from then on became the family's principal seat. It was this decision that helped to ensure that the main structure of the house built at Cotehele by Sir Richard and Sir Piers would survive with so little alteration.

THE BUILDING OF THE HOUSE

Hidden among the woods above the Calstock reach of the River Tamar, Cotehele seems remote from the modern world. Architecturally, time also appears to have stood still, thanks largely to the remarkably unaltered state of the house and the durability of the local granite and slatestone out of which it is built. Although other important manor houses in Cornwall – Roscarrock in St Endellion parish, Tonacombe in Morwenstow and the unfinished and abandoned complex at Trecarrel in Lezant – share

some of its qualities, Cotehele is unique in showing few obvious signs of rebuilding since the mid-seventeenth century. The decision by the Edgcumbes to build a new family seat in the mid 1500s relieved Cotehele of most of the pressures of changing fashion and standards of comfort that alter and shape any house in full use over the centuries. In spite of the move to Mount Edgcumbe, Cotehele was not allowed to fall into dereliction, nor was it sold out of the family and reduced by partial demolition to farmhouse size, the fate of some ancient manor houses in the South West.

The local materials out of which Cotehele is constructed create its strongly regional character. The house is built of brown and grey slatestone rubble, ubiquitous in Cornwall, with some granite ashlar masonry and dressings. Neither material takes a fine finish. Slatestone is quarried only in small blocks and, whether used in local churches or farmhouses, has an inevitably homespun quality. The sheer intractable hardness of granite gives a rustic quality to any carved detail, and even at its

The south range

finest, on the church of St Mary Magdalene at Launceston, the effect is robust rather than delicate.

The present house incorporates parts of the fabric of the medieval house of the de Cotehele family, which was transformed in the late fifteenth and sixteenth centuries by the Edgcumbes – principally Sir Richard and his son, Sir Piers – into a complex triple-court-plan house. The appearance of the pre-Tudor house and the precise extent to which its old walls and plan were retained by subsequent generations of the Edgcumbe family has been the subject of a recent study, which can be viewed at the property.

Sir Richard Edgcumbe is certainly unlikely to have undertaken a programme of mass demolition and building afresh – this would have been neither convenient nor thrifty. Old walling and parts of the earlier building that could be remodelled to new standards of convenience and status would have been retained. The siting of the old Cotehele mansion also played an important part in determining the plan of the new Edgcumbe house.

The arrangement is inward-looking, the main ranges opening on to enclosed courts with only small windows in the outer walls, suggesting a semi-defensive function. This characteristic may originate from pre-Tudor times, but many equally have been a response to the unstable politics of Cornwall in the late fifteenth and sixteenth centuries. Contemporary documents chart the lawlessness of great landowners in the county in the late fifteenth century, and there were Cornish rebellions in 1497, 1548 and 1549. Fluctuations in the tin trade throughout the period also posed threats to security, and as late as 1568 the West Country tin miners were described as a 'rough and mutinous multitude'. The Edgcumbes held Crown appointments. Sir Piers, for instance, was one of the members of the Council in the West, which was created to bring the West Country more firmly under royal control. They were wise, therefore, to establish a secure house at Cotehele.

The Chapel is likely to have been the first project in the major rebuilding of Cotehele by Sir Richard and Sir Piers. A chapel at Cotehele was licensed as early as 1411 and there may have been one before that date. It stood on the same site as today's chapel, and was massively rebuilt by Sir Piers in the early

sixteenth century. The barrel-vaulted type of roof construction in the Chapel is found in countless other late medieval church roofs in Devon and Cornwall. The ornate granite bellcote over the west end is of Breton influence, and is similar to the bellcote on the chapel of St Mary at South Zeal on the northern fringe of Dartmoor, and the holy well at Dupath near Callington is crowned with a similar but simplified version.

After the Chapel the next phase in the programme of rebuilding Cotehele was the adjoining north range, which dates from the early sixteenth century, although it may represent a recasting of an earlier building on the same site. The abrupt juxtaposition of the walls in the north-west corner marks an obvious transition between the building of the Chapel and the north range, which contains the Hall, rising through two storeys, to the east and, alongside at the higher end, a cross-wing containing the Parlour (now the Old Dining Room) with the Solar (principal chamber; now South and Red Rooms) above. The granite ashlar used on the exterior marks out the superior status of these rooms, and the Hall door frame, positioned in line with the gatehouse entrance, is designed to impress the visitor with its distinctive carved granite tympanum, matching that of the gatehouse. The studded oak folding door to the Hall also deserves attention. It is a fine piece of sixteenth-century craftsmanship and just one of the many carpentry and joinery features that give Cotehele the authentic textures and surfaces of the Tudor period.

The Hall is the showpiece of Cotehele. The upper or dais end is lit by a deep mullioned and transomed granite window, glazed with the usual small panes of leaded glass. On the opposite wall is a massive moulded granite fireplace. The end of the Hall where the lord sat was therefore well served for light and warmth.

High above is the spectacular roof – seven bays of arch-braced trusses, the feet of the principal rafters curving down to the wall in the local cruck tradition. Each bay contains tiers of intersecting wind-braces. Although technically the arch-braces give added support to the trusses and the wind-braces provide longitudinal strength between the trusses, they are moulded and treated decoratively, since

The Chapel was probably the first part of Cotehele rebuilt by Sir Piers Edgcumbe; watercolour by Nicholas Condy, c.1840 (City of Plymouth Museum & Art Gallery)

The arch-braced roof of the Hall is a particularly fine example of early sixteenth-century Cornish craftsmanship; watercolour by Nicholas Condy, c.1840 (City of Plymouth Museum & Art Gallery)

show was as much a consideration as strength. The basic arch-braced form of the roof is traditional to the South West and survives in houses of a much lower status than Cotehele. It is the quality and richness of the wind-bracing that distinguishes the Cotehele roof from its contemporaries. Only Trecarrel and Wortham, the home of the Dinham family in Lifton parish, west Devon, survive with similar ornamented wind-bracing.

The layout at the lower end of the Hall at Cotehele is unconventional. The end wall contains three service doorways which, in a conventional plan, would lead to the Kitchen, Pantry and Buttery. Here, one leads to the Kitchen, it is likely that the second would originally have led to a grand staircase giving access to the principal rooms on the first floor, and the third leads to the service rooms on the ground floor.

The Kitchen is offset from the Hall, an unusual position, although not unprecedented and probably a consequence of the geography of the site, which

slopes sharply away to the east. This arrangement also had the advantage of allowing reasonable access from the Kitchen, across the service court, to the private rooms in the cross-wing by means of the door at the front of the staircase. More unusual is the direct entry into the body of the Hall. Most hall-houses have a cross-passage between opposing front and back doorways at the lower end, screened off from the main hall. The absence of such a screens passage is probably a product of the relatively late date and perhaps infrequent use of the Hall.

In architectural terms, the Hall at Cotehele is a late example in a long tradition of open halls for which evidence can be found in almost every surviving medieval house. The main distinction between the sixteenth-century Hall at Cotehele and earlier medieval halls is one of usage. In the medieval period the hall was the focus of a communal way of life, often being used not only for eating and entertaining, but also serving as a kitchen and sleeping quarters as well. By the sixteenth century the lord and his family lived at a greater distance from the other members of their household. As a result, private apartments, set aside for this purpose, became increasingly grand and extensive. This was a general change, lamented as early as the late fourteenth century by the poet William Langland, who recognised that the new remoteness of the master of the house was not merely occasioned by architectural fashion, but had its social consequences:

Wretched is the hall, each day in the week,
There neither lord nor lady liketh now to sit.
The rich now have a rule to eat by themselves
In a private parlour, in despite of poor men,
Or in a chamber with a chimney, and leave the great
    hall
That was made for meals, for men to eat in
So that any spilled food was spare for another.

The relationship between the Hall and the cross-wing, which Sir Piers Edgcumbe added at the west end in the early sixteenth century to contain his private apartments, reveals the increasing emphasis on the privacy of the family in Tudor times. Externally the gable end of the cross-wing, facing out over the main court, emulates the grandeur of the Hall, with its ashlar masonry and large mullioned and transomed windows. Internally, the cross-wing was conceived on terms of almost equal status with the Hall. Not only were the rooms themselves – the Parlour below and the Solar above – of generous size, served by good fireplaces and lit by large windows, but the Solar was given an arch-braced roof with moulded wind-bracing comparable to that of the Hall. (The Solar roof is concealed by a later ceiling and is not on public view.)

The early sixteenth-century programme also included alterations to the south and east ranges. The south range masonry shows that the imposing, crenellated ashlar granite gatehouse has been cut into earlier slatestone rubble. Parallels to the carved granite tympanum, matching that of the Hall door, can be found at Week St Mary Grammar School in

The richly carved oak armchair in the Hall was assembled in the nineteenth century from earlier pieces

north Cornwall, founded in 1506, and at Wortham in Devon. Most of the sixteenth-century internal plan and features of the east range were altered in 1862, when extensive remodelling took place in a style sympathetic to the Tudor character of the building.

Sadly, little evidence has survived of how the house was furnished in Tudor times. We can only fall back on comparative scholarship to imagine a house with a few precious panels of tapestry, perhaps a carpet draped over a table, and a collection of oak beds, tables, forms and stools. Some of the pieces of furniture that would have adorned Tudor Cotehele survive only as fragments incorporated into the 'antiquarian' furniture of the eighteenth and nineteenth centuries, such as the armchair with the Renaissance medallion as its back panel.

THE SEVENTEENTH AND EIGHTEENTH CENTURIES

What kind of household remained at Cotehele in the late sixteenth century after the building of the Mount Edgcumbe House is still a matter of conjecture, as many of the family records were destroyed during the Second World War. The family may have continued living there, or perhaps it was occupied by dependent relatives, or by a steward carrying out estate administration.

In 1554 Sir Richard Edgcumbe (c.1499–1562) held a splendid party at Mount Edgcumbe for the Admirals of the English, Spanish and Flanders navies, who were in Plymouth preparing for the marriage of Queen Mary and Philip of Spain. Affectionately known as 'the good old knight of the castle', he was renowned as a good housekeeper, always ensuring that he had two years of provisions in hand of all things necessary for himself and his family, and keeping £100 in cash for his current needs. In his youth he was interested in astrology and the occult, and in his latter years had to keep a private chaplain to prove his orthodoxy in this troubled period of religious conflict.

Sir Richard added the Retainers' Court buildings, the Gatehouse Tower and the North West Tower to Cotehele. The latter was an economical piece of planning. It could serve either as a suite of inner retiring rooms beyond the Parlour cross-wing or as an independent unit within the Cotehele complex. The increasing demands for privacy and comfort must have led to the need for smaller rooms, and in particular for more bedrooms, and incorporating these into a tower was a sensible way of adding to the building since the rising ground to the north would have made it difficult to extend the house for any length in this direction.

His heir, Piers (by 1536–1607/8), was the fourth generation of the family to sit in Parliament and became Sheriff of Devon. He married Margaret Luttrell, a member of another famous West Country family and had nine children. One of these, Margaret, was Queen Elizabeth I's favourite Maid of Honour and correspondent of Sir Philip Sidney. Satirised as a Puritan in his youth, Piers Edgcumbe was an active MP until his later years, when the cost

Margaret, Lady Denny, daughter of the Sir Piers Edgcumbe who owned Cotehele in the late sixteenth century. She was the favourite Maid of Honour of Elizabeth I. Painted c.1620 (City of Plymouth Museum & Art Gallery, Mount Edgcumbe House Collection)

of exploiting the mines on his estate proved a considerable drain on his resources. In 1598 Christopher Harris remarked that 'he goes seldom from his house'.

Sir Piers was succeeded by two of his sons, Piers and then Sir Richard (1563–1639), who was knighted at the Coronation of James I in 1603. By his judicious marriages Sir Richard did much to repair the financial health of the Edgcumbe estates. His first wife, Anne Cary, was described by her sister-in-law as 'a good housewife and very wary in her expenses'. In 1608 he married Mary Coteel, the daughter of Sir Thomas Coteel, a Flemish merchant.

Despite the move to Mount Edgcumbe, Cotehele was added to and improved in the seventeenth century.

At the outset of the Civil War in the 1640s, Cotehele was occupied by Col. Piers Edgcumbe (c.1610–67), a Royalist supporter. His home at Mount Edgcumbe was uncomfortably close to the Parliamentarian stronghold of Plymouth and he therefore moved his family and household back to Cotehele for reasons of safety and spent the rest of his life there. The fines he had incurred for his support of the King may have limited his budget for alterations to Cotehele. Nevertheless in the 1650s he replaced the main staircase, which was originally a winding newel stair, with the existing straight flights of timber steps, which necessitated alterations to the existing rooms on the ground floor.

A description of these improvements appears in the earliest building accounts for Cotehele, dated 1651–2. The anonymous builder who was responsible for the work provided plans of the Parlour cross-wing with a letter of commentary on the progress and difficulties of the alterations, principally the new 'great stairs'. This is not only full of practical detail, but its tone suggests a patron who definitely knew his own mind and kept a close eye on the work:

I know that you do much dislike winding steps, I confess Square ones be better when they can [be] had . . . . This is so much as I can express to you in writing . . . but true satisfaction I cannot give you in the particular except you were here of which I have good hope.

The north-west tower was probably added in the 1550s by Richard Edgcumbe (c.1499–1562); watercolour by Nicholas Condy, c.1840 (City of Plymouth Museum & Art Gallery)

The letter gives an insight into the taste of a mid-seventeenth-century owner attempting to refine an earlier dwelling. His desire to provide the cross-wing with a more commodious main stair, and another, undated scheme (apparently never executed) for wall-panelling are entirely in accordance with the fashion of the time. More unexpected is the information in a further document at the Cornwall County Record Office that old windows at Cotehele were being reused and re-sited. Reference is made to a window in the Little Parlour 'that is polled downe and to be converted for a window in the Great Parlour'. The reuse of timber and masonry in new structures had occurred for centuries, but at this date it was certainly not general practice to reuse old windows in the remodelling of

principal rooms. The re-siting of old features and, as the documents show, even the design of new windows with very similar profiles to the old ones, may suggest an appreciation of the value and integrity of the old architecture of the house at a surprisingly early date, but it may simply indicate frugality or lack of money.

After Col. Edgcumbe's death, the Edgcumbes spent more time at the modern and comfortable house at Mount Edgcumbe. Col. Edgcumbe's loyalty to the Crown was not forgotten, for his son, Richard (1640–88), was knighted at the Restoration and entertained the King twice at Mount Edgcumbe, in 1671 and 1677. In 1671 he married Lady Anne Montagu, who mysteriously 'died' in 1675, as Richard Polwhele, the historian of Devon and Cornwall, relates:

The family were then residing at Cuteel. Lady Edgcumbe had expired: in consequence of what disorder I am not informed. Her body was deposited in the family vault not I suppose in less than a week after her supposed death. The interment, however, had not long taken place, before the sexton, from a motive sufficiently obvious went down into the vault; and observing a gold-ring on her Ladyship's finger, attempted to draw it off; but not succeeding, pressed and pinched the finger – when the body very sensibly moved in the coffin. The man ran off in terror, leaving his lanthorn behind him. Her Ladyship arose, and taking the lanthorn, proceeded to the mansion house. It was about five years after, that ... her [son], Sir Richard was born.

In 1742, this Sir Richard (1680–1758), for many years MP for St Germans and later for Plympton, a Lord of the Treasury, Paymaster-General for Ireland and Chancellor of the Duchy of Lancaster, was created Baron Edgcumbe of Mount Edgcumbe. He was a friend and supporter of the Prime Minister, Sir Robert Walpole, and managed many Cornish pocket boroughs in his interest. At this time the Duchy returned 44 members, whilst there were only 42 for the whole of Scotland, so Edgcumbe's support was worth a good deal. Edgcumbe was raised to the peerage following Walpole's fall from power, in order, their opponents suggested, to avoid an interrogation which might further disgrace the outgoing Prime Minister. He was also a particular favourite of George II, according to some authorities, because he was even shorter than that diminutive monarch.

John Cornforth has suggested that in the 1730s the 1st Baron Edgcumbe may have been responsible for fitting up the principal rooms with the late seventeenth-century tapestries, more or less in the positions that they occupy today. If this is the case, it is an early example of the revival of ancient interiors that was to become so popular in the late eighteenth and early nineteenth centuries.

Family tradition records that the 1st Baron Edgcumbe was the discoverer of the Plympton-born artist Joshua Reynolds, who as a boy of twelve was on a visit to Mount Edgcumbe:

... and on a certain Sunday was at Maker Church with the 1st Lord Edgcumbe and his son. It was noticed that the two boys were misbehaving themselves during the sermon, and when they returned to the house after the service his Lordship sent for his son, and took him to task for his misconduct. The boy's defence was that

Reynolds had drawn such a capital likeness of the vicar on his thumb-nail that they could not stop themselves laughing. The culprit was summoned, and produced the miniature on his nail. After admonishing the young artist with as serious a face as he could command, Lord Edgcumbe ordered him not to wash his hands till the next day, and then giving him a boat house at Cremill [Cremyll] for his studio, a piece of boat-sail for canvas and a few common paints, he set him to make a copy of his first sketch from the life.

Although the story is not authenticated, later in life Sir Joshua Reynolds certainly did paint the 1st Baron Edgcumbe with his dog, of which Lord Edgcumbe was so fond that after its death the skeleton was mounted in the Garden House at Mount Edgcumbe, where he used to go to talk to it.

The 2nd Baron Edgcumbe, his eldest son Richard (1716–61), after a career in the Army also entered Parliament, becoming a Lord of the Admiralty in 1753 and Controller of His Majesty's Household three years later. He was an aesthete, poet and wit, and a friend of George Selwyn, Gilly Williams and Horace Walpole, three of the choicest spirits of the age. He was a friend and patron of Reynolds like his father, and an accomplished draughtsman, as Walpole testifies; his skill 'is said to have been such as might entitle him to a place in the Anecdotes of English Painting, while the ease and harmony of his poetic productions gave him an authorised introduction here'. He was, Walpole goes on to say, 'a man of fine parts, great knowledge and original wit, who possessed a light and easy vein of poetry: who was calculated by nature to serve the public and to charm society.' But, unfortunately, this gifted individual 'was a man of pleasure, and left his gay associates a most affecting example of how health, fame, ambition and everything that may be laudable in principle or practice are drawn into and absorbed by that most destructive of all whirlpools – gaming.' In his youth he gambled away 20 guineas a day at White's, and was only rescued by a political ally, Henry Pelham, who secured for him a secret service pension of £500 a year.

A year after this charming and popular character succeeded to his title in 1758, he received the first royal visitor recorded at Cotehele. *The London*

Chronicle or Universal Evening Post of 28–31 July 1759 relates some 'Country News':

Saltash July 24 1759 – On Saturday last his Royal Highness Prince Edward [later Duke of York] went up the Tamar from Mount Edgcumbe with Lord Edgcumbe and several other persons of distinction, in six or eight boats, as far as the water would bear them, towards the Salmon Weir at Calstock. The water failing, horses were procured from the neighbourhood, and his Royal Highness and Lord Edgcumbe rode about a mile from the landing place to the Weir where twenty salmon were caught. A cold collation was conveyed from the Mount to Cothill (the ancient seat of the Edgcumbes on the Cornish side of the Tamar) to regale the company on their return.

Despite fathering four children by his mistress Mrs Ann Franks, the 2nd Baron did not marry her, and so was succeeded as 3rd Baron Edgcumbe by his brother George in 1761. In the same year George married Emma Gilbert, the daughter of the Archbishop of York, and in the following year became a Rear-Admiral. The 3rd Baron Edgcumbe (1720/1–95) had entered the navy as a young midshipman, and spent long periods away from Cotehele at sea, seeing much action in the troubled years of the mid-eighteenth century. During the 3rd Baron's spell as Commander-in-Chief in Plymouth

(1766–70), the explorer Captain Cook set sail in the *Endeavour* for the South Pacific. Perhaps in recognition of the 3rd Baron's fine hospitality Cook named two mountains after him (in New Zealand and Alaska), and an Edgcumbe Bay in Australia.

In 1781 a royal party visited Mount Edgcumbe and George was created 1st Viscount Mount Edgcumbe and Valletort – some said in recognition of the sacrifice he had made two years earlier by felling many trees in the park at Mount Edgcumbe for the use of the navy. On another western progress, in 1789, when George III and Queen Charlotte also visited Cotehele, he was created 1st Earl of Mount Edgcumbe. The Queen has left us a particularly vivid account of this visit:

… landed at the woods of Cotehill ½ hour after 10 where we found Lrd & Ldy Mount Edgcumbe ready to receive Us. We went in their Coach up to this Old Family seat of theirs where His Ancestors lived at least 200 Years before they had Mount Edgcumbe. It did originally exist of 3 Courts, of which there is now but one existing & Consists of a large Hall full of Old Armor & Swords & Old Carved Chairs of the Times, a Drawing Room Hung with Old Tapestry, the Scirtingboard of which is straw the Chair Seats made of the Priests Vestments. A Chapel which is still in good repair. The Window painted Glass but damaged & defaced. A small Bed Chamber, 2 Closets & a Dressing-

The 'Out-of-Town' Party: Richard, 2nd Baron Edgcumbe (on right), with his friends George Selwyn (standing) and Gilly Williams (behind). Painted in 1759 by Sir Joshua Reynolds for their mutual friend, Horace Walpole (City of Bristol Museum & Art Gallery)

Richard, 2nd Baron Edgcumbe; by Sir Joshua Reynolds, 1748 (City of Plymouth Museum & Art Gallery, Mount Edgcumbe House Collection)

room all Hung with Old Tapestry. Above stairs there is a Drawingroom The Chairs Black Ebony Carved & a Cabinet the same, & 4 Bedchambers all Hung the Same. At Breakfast we Eat off the Old Family Pewter, & used Silver knives Forks & Spoons which have been Time immemorial in the Family & have always been kept at this place. The Decanters are of the year 1646 the name of the Wines burnt in the Earthenware for that Time Wines were sold at the Apothecaries Shop & in Sending such a Decanter it was filled with the Wine it bore the Label off. The Desert Plates are Old Delph of a very large Size but make no part of the Old Family Furniture. We embarked again 10 minutes after 12.

Surprisingly for an admiral, the 1st Earl had both scientific and antiquarian interests, being a Fellow of the Royal Society and the Society of Antiquaries, and, like his brother, a friend of Horace Walpole. The 1st Earl shared the family's fascination with Cotehele and its history. He restored Sir Richard Edgcumbe's Chapel in the Wood in 1769 and may have introduced the picture of Sir Richard's tomb at

Morlaix now in the Chapel in the house, together with the Gothick blind fretwork on the Chapel screen. John Cornforth has argued that he bought suitably old furniture to increase the romantic appeal at Cotehele. He has also suggested that he acquired the elaborately turned ebony seat furniture in the Old Drawing Room on which George III and Queen Charlotte allegedly sat when they breakfasted at Cotehele. Such furniture, as Clive Wainwright has shown, was avidly sought by members of Walpole's circle, who regarded it, mistakenly, as of Tudor origin. That Cotehele and its contents were exciting widespread interest from the antiquarian-minded by the late eighteenth century is clear from several contemporary references, not least Horace Walpole, who wrote in 1777 with jokey exaggeration, 'I never did see Cotehel, and am sorry. Is not the old wardrobe there still? There is one from the time of Cain, but Adam's breeches and Eve's under-petticoat were eaten by a goat in the ark.'

SINCE 1800

Richard, 2nd Earl of Mount Edgcumbe (1764–1839) was, like his father, a member of the Society of Antiquaries, but seems to have been a less earnest individual – a keen amateur actor, the composer of an opera, *Zenobia*, produced at the King's Theatre, London, in 1800, and the author of a much-reprinted account of *Musical Reminiscences of an old Amateur chiefly respecting Italian Opera in England 1773 to 1823* (1825). He was, according to Cyrus Redding, 'a mere fribble, exhibiting little above the calibre of an opera connoisseur, with something of the mimic…'. He seldom visited Cotehele, except in the summer, when he is said to have lived in an Elizabethan manner. His wife, Lady Sophia Hobart, daughter of the Earl of Buckinghamshire, brought with her a great deal of property at Bere Ferrers on the Devon bank of the Tamar, and much increased the size of the family estate. According to the 4th Earl of Mount Edgcumbe's *Records of the Edgcumbe Family*, 'For many years Cotehele was rarely visited by the family and was left in the care of a farmer and his wife, under whose regime the arms in the hall are said to have received a coat of brown paint

Richard, 2nd Earl of Mount Edgcumbe was a keen amateur actor. In this 1803 caricature by James Gillray, he appears in the left foreground rehearsing with other members of the Picnic Society

every seven years, and the pictures a wash of gin and water every spring and fall'.

The 3rd Earl, Ernest Augustus (1797–1861), was an aide-de-camp to Queen Victoria, and received her and Prince Albert at Cotehele during their Western Cruise in 1846. Two years later he was travelling in Europe where he witnessed the revolutions in Palermo and Rome. He published accounts of these journeys and some of the speeches he made in the House of Lords.

In 1840 the Rev. F. V. J. Arundell, rector of the nearby parish of Landulph, dedicated his account of Cotehele to the 3rd Earl, with lithographs after a series of watercolours of Cotehele by the Plymouth artist Nicholas Condy, who signed the Cotehele Visitors' Book in 1836. (An album of some similar watercolours was acquired by Queen Adelaide, wife of William IV, and is now in the Plymouth City Museum.) Mr Arundell's text is heavily laced with the spirit of romantic antiquarianism, as its opening sentences make clear:

It is comparatively but a short time ago when mansion after mansion, possessing even the interest of Cotehele, was suffered to crumble into ruin or taken down to make way for modern erections. Happily that Vandal spirit is arrested, and there is now as eager a search for buildings that have the smallest pretensions to antiquity, and as anxious a desire to save them from further destruction, as there is for every article of furniture, and for every fragment of ancient carved work, which may be supposed to have existed in these mansions of early days.

That the author was no furniture historian is revealed by his next, and not unexpected, remark that 'all the rooms retain their ancient furniture, and the latest not more modern than the reign of Elizabeth'. It is with some caution therefore that one approaches the illustrations for the book. Some of the rooms are filled with strange combinations of people – medieval knights and Stuart cavaliers mingling with characters in contemporary dress –

45

and one might suspect that the furniture has been 'rearranged' to accommodate these imaginary figures into convincing compositions. In fact, however, the artist has focused his attention minutely on the rooms themselves and what is inside them, and the rendering of carved woodwork, patterned textiles, even the subject-matter of the tapestries, is done with remarkable accuracy and an almost clinical detachment, which gives the rooms a curiously inhospitable appearance. In short, there is little reason to suppose that the forces of romantic nostalgia have blurred the artist's vision from a faithful record of the appearance of the rooms at that time.

In 1853 the 3rd Earl built a handsome 'marine residence' known as the Winter Villa. This large house stood opposite Mount Edgcumbe and the family would often stay there for a short season when the Fleet was in, or when Assemblies were being held in Plymouth, and thus avoid a possibly rough crossing of the estuary at night.

On the 3rd Earl's death in 1861 his widow, Caroline Augusta, who was to live for another twenty years, decided that she would like to settle at Cotehele, where no member of the family had lived – other than for short periods – since Col. Piers Edgcumbe had died there in 1667. A major building programme was then put in hand, and Cotehele was awakened from 200 years of comparative slumber. The principal change was in the east range. This had hitherto consisted on the ground floor of a large butler's pantry, entered from the east end of the Hall, with beer and wine cellars beyond, and on the first floor of servants' bedchambers ill-lit by tiny windows. This range was now to become the living quarters of the Dowager Countess.

The work was carried out with unusual respect for the architectural uniformity of the house. A two-storeyed bay was added: the porch on the ground floor, which is dated 1862, became the principal entrance of the house; the window above flooded with light a big new drawing-room on the first floor with a beautiful view down the valley to the Calstock reach of the River Tamar below.

On the ground floor a large dining-room led off from the north side of the staircase hall (connected to the original kitchen of the old house), with a library on the south side. Upstairs there were new bedrooms and dressing-rooms. At the north-east angle of the house, where formerly there were tumbledown outbuildings and a 'wood hole', a comfortable, two-storey cottage was added for the butler and his wife. The modernisation allowed the Countess to live in centrally heated comfort, though all her rooms still had large open fireplaces.

An album of early photographs of West Country houses includes views of the interior of Cotehele in about 1860, just before the decision to revive the house for contemporary living. These show that although apparently in occupation, the old rooms were still sparsely furnished by the standards of the time, although the arrangements were 'looser' than those recorded by Condy 20 years previously and more cluttered than they appear today. Other photographs taken in the 1870s and '80s serve to show that considerable changes had by then taken place in the arrangement and function of rooms within the core of the old house. Nevertheless, the old rooms remained essentially uncluttered because

Ernest Augustus, 3rd Earl of Mount Edgcumbe; by F. Lane after James Sant (City of Plymouth Museum & Art Gallery, Mount Edgcumbe House Collection)

The 3rd Earl's wife, Caroline Augusta Feilding, with their two youngest children; by James Sant. After her husband's death in 1861 she decided to settle at Cotehele, where the family had not lived permanently since the seventeenth century (City of Plymouth Museum & Art Gallery, Mount Edgcumbe House Collection)

there appears to have been very little new furniture introduced to supplement the older pieces.

The revival of Cotehele seemed likely to come to an end on the Countess's death, but another similarly happy period was to follow. Her unmarried daughter, Lady Ernestine Edgcumbe, continued to live in the house. She appears to have been something of a tartar, keeping up considerable state, being driven to St Dominick church in a carriage with cockaded footmen. The old servants who were still at Cotehele when the National Trust acquired it in 1947 remembered her well. Lady Ernestine lived at Cotehele for over 20 years, moving in about 1905 to live at Honicombe, another house belonging to the family, next to Buddles Adit

– where she had 'first pull' on the Cotehele water supply. She lived at Honicombe until her death in 1925.

Her brother, William Henry, 4th Earl of Mount Edgcumbe (1832–1917), was a considerable figure in the county. Much preferring Cornwall to London, he was a good landlord, taking pleasure in the management of the extensive Edgcumbe estates. With Lord St Levan of St Michael's Mount, he was the owner of the 'Halfpenny Bridge', the toll bridge which connected Plymouth to Devonport and brought in a handsome revenue every year. Travellers, however, found this a great burden, as every foot passenger, except for soldiers, had to pay the toll. This was particularly resented by the many sailors in the port, where from at least 1850 it is recorded that after mess they sang the following song:

Lordy Edgcumbe, Lord divine
All the Hakey fish are thine;
All the fishes in the sea
Noble Lord belong to thee.

Lordy Edgcumbe, we are told
That you've bags and bags of gold;
So lift the Toll, for this is true,
What's much for us is nought for you.

Lordy Edgcumbe, up the hill,
'Tis a shame to treat us ill;
Marines and soldiers go through free,
Then why the b----- h--- can't we?

As well as being Lord Lieutenant of Cornwall and holding many active or honorary offices, the 4th Earl was the first Chairman of the County Council, from 1898 until his death in 1917, and President of the Council for the building of Truro Cathedral. He was a friend of the Prince of Wales, and accompanied him on his trips abroad. He was also Lord Chamberlain in 1879–80 and Lord Steward in 1885–6. His first wife, Lady Katherine Hamilton, daughter of the Duke of Abercorn, died in 1874, and 32 years later he married his cousin, Caroline Cecilia, previously the Countess of Ravensworth. The 4th Earl was his family's historian and put in order and then catalogued the enormous number of family muniments (many destroyed when Mount Edgcumbe was bombed in 1941).

The 6th Earl and Countess of Mount Edgcumbe in their coronation robes, by Mills, 1953 (Plymouth City Museum & Art Gallery, Mount Edgcumbe House Collection)

He was succeeded as 5th Earl by his son, Piers (1865–1944), who served in the Boer War and then busied himself with local affairs, though on a lesser scale than his father had done. He was widowed in 1935, and having been bombed out of Mount Edgcumbe, he came to live at Cotehele. His obituary in the local paper read:

So Passes a Bit of England.... The Fifth Earl of Mount Edgcumbe was one of the old-fashioned earls – old-fashioned in the best sense.... But war, and the death of the master has broken up the big household just as it has done many another.... The London house in Belgrave Square has been closed since early in the war.... The pleasure gardens of the estate in Cornwall are taken over by the military.... The yacht has been laid up since the war.... The kitchen garden is producing food which is marketed.... The woodmen are carrying out their work for the Government.

His cousin, Kenelm Edgcumbe (1873–1965), became 6th Earl. He was an eminent electrical engineer, the founder of the Everett Edgcumbe Company in 1900, and in 1927 President of the Institute of Electrical Engineers. Tragically, he had lost his only son, Piers, in action at Dunkirk in May 1940, but he was determined to play his part in the restoration of the family home. He and his wife came to live at Cotehele while a house was being converted for them in the stables at Mount Edgcumbe. He then devoted himself to rebuilding the main house, completing it in 1960 at the age of 87.

Upon succeeding to the family estate, he had suggested to the Treasury that the Cotehele property of almost 1,300 acres should be accepted in part-payment of the 5th Earl's death duties, and handed over to the National Trust. This was done in 1947, and Cotehele became the first house and estate to be acquired by the Trust through the National Land Fund. The Trust is deeply indebted both to the Treasury and to the 6th Earl of Mount Edgcumbe whose persistence and patient negotiation established an invaluable precedent. He died in 1965, and the family trustees generously continued to leave on loan in the state rooms all the tapestries, armour and furniture. In 1974 most of these contents were, in their turn, given to the Trust by the Treasury, which had accepted them in lieu of estate duty on the death of the 6th Earl.

Edward Piers Edgcumbe, a distant cousin from New Zealand, succeeded as 7th Earl in 1965 and divided his time between Mount Edgcumbe and his sheep farm in New Zealand. His nephew, Robert Charles, is the present and 8th Earl of Mount Edgcumbe. He has five daughters and also spends part of the year in Britain and part in the Antipodes.